"Just imagine if you went to a professional sports event, a theater production, or an ice skating performance and those who are participating never bothered to practice. How would you feel? My bet is that you would most likely want your money back. Well, that is just how many employees feel when they've been requested to take valuable time away from what they do to attend a training event, and the individual assigned to run the session is poorly prepared."

Thom Mindala

Once any training initiative or program has been successfully created and made ready to be implemented, the most important task now is to be prepared to present it professionally and efficiently. I have another favorite saying, which is: "when a company asks employees to take time out of their busy schedules to participate in training sessions, they owe it to them to make sure the session is presented in an efficient, professional, and dynamic manner." And, this is true whether the training is to be delivered in a classroom setting, by way of a webinar, on Video CDs, on an LMS platform, or even by way of self study materials.

While each one of the subjects we cover in this "Winning Presentations Publication" has in fact had volumes of text written and is available from many sources, our goal is to condense the discussion for ready use specifically by the business manager who's not a professional presenter so he or she can prepare a quality training presentation. More to the point, this "Winning Presentations Publication" is specifically intended to help you do so in a quick, efficient, and easy to identify manner.

I should note before we move forward with our discussion that when it comes to making presentations the internet is an awesome and valuable resource that shouldn't be ignored. The internet is a wonderful place to go for detailed information on virtually any subject, and is also a great place to find many of the pictures and graphics you might want to use in your presentations. You only need to be very careful that you don't tread on copyright laws when you do so. Plagiarism is something that we must always avoid as professionals and when we unnecessarily trounce all over copyright laws we are in fact plagiarizing somebody else's work. I have 4 rules that I live by to avoid doing so:

> RULE #1: Always give credit to the source for any quotes I use.

> RULE #2: If the "R" copyright symbol is visible, I shouldn't copy it.

> RULE #3: Ask yourself... is the material to be used internally or externally?

> RULE #4: If you aren't sure... don't use it.

Stay on top of this sticky issue and you will never have to worry about a call from your legal team (or worse, somebody else's). But if you do have a question and have a legal department to rely on, be sure to do so before you move forward.

What are *TRAIN2WIN* Publications?

TRAIN2WIN Publications is a series of easy to use training tools which are designed to help define the subject content in a manner that allows the reader to fully understand the information in a way that will help establish the basis for a functional training initiative or program. While not intended to be a complete analysis or study of the identified subject, each book in the *TRAIN2WIN* Publication series provides a detailed overview.

Each *TRAIN2WIN* Publication may be used as a presentation / instructor guide, or can be used as an informational style handout piece for those taking a training course. Each Publication addresses a unique and particular training subject, and is written in easy to read and understand language.

Each pamphlet in the *TRAIN2WIN* Publications Series is supported by a companion Power Point Presentation that can be ordered for a small additional fee by contacting us directly at *TRAIN2WIN* by telephone (303-947-8989), by email (TMindala@gmail.com), or by simply contacting us on our website (Train2win.weebly.com) to send us a request. Each Publication is also available to download in Stick Drive by contacting *TRAIN2WIN.*

Winning
Presentations

Contents

Contrary to what we might assume, folks like Tom Hanks, Brad Pitt, and Meryl Streep were not born with the skills of accomplished actors and actresses. They may have had an innate ability to get in front of people, but in each case it has taken many years of hard work to learn their craft.

So, let's ask ourselves... will it take some hard work to learn to be a better and more professional instructor and presenter? You bet it will. But, should it take years and years of effort to refine those skills? No, it shouldn't and here's the reason. Where a Hollywood performer must rely on perfection in front of a camera to be successful with a paying audience, this just isn't the case with business professionals who are providing instruction or making presentations to their peers and subordinates. I will note here that this isn't the case for a paid consultant and also will say up front that the better your skills are the better your results will be from those you instruct or present to. I sometimes refer to it as: "you only need to be well organized, entirely versed in the subject matter, and dynamic enough with the presentation to hold the interest of the group." Doesn't seem like much does it.

Seriously though, if you commit yourself to becoming a well organized instructor who knows his or her material hands down, then works to become dynamic and interesting to his or her "customers" I will guarantee to you that they will forgive you for not being perfect. No, you don't have to have the skill of a Hollywood actor or actress, but you do need to have the ability to present yourself well, manage the systems for the presentation you are making, and manage the room while you keep things interesting for those you invite to train.

I call it "being credible" and it really starts with the fact that regardless what skills you learn or what ideas you get from others to use, you must simply be yourself. Yes, you need to have some specific skills that ensure that your presentation is what it needs to be to be relevant and hold the attention of your audience, but if you try to be anything other than yourself, you will ultimately fail. And, here's what I mean. If you're a person who is a casual dresser, you don't all of a sudden show up in a tuxedo to make a presentation. Likewise, if you aren't comfortable doing so, you shouldn't start cracking jokes to the group.

For example, I'm a guy who tends to want to engage the group I'm instructing or speaking to, so my first priority is to always learn as much about them as I can so that I can determine who my allies are and who I might need to give some special attention to in order to get them on my side. To do so, I will often create a session opening "ice breaker" designed to get the information I need to come back to later. Also, I tend to be a story teller when I present. So, I'm always on the lookout for relevant stories which help make my points. Lastly, I love to poke fun at myself and to a degree the participants in the room to keep things lively and fun. These are no more than the things I am and what works for me and my style.

There are no fool proof methods that are guaranteed to work in every situation, but you will need to develop a "style" that allows you to use the various skills and techniques we will talk about and those you gather from others to incorporate into your own way of doing things as a presenter / instructor. **Your chosen style is an important consideration and will be essential to your success.**

And what exactly do we mean by style? We mean it's how you look, how you act, how you relate, and how you respond to the group you are presenting to. It involves everything from the clothes you wear, how you set up the room, where you stand, how you use your hands, and just how you plan to engage the group during the session. These all need to fit into what your personal style is to the point that you do them without having to give them a second's thought.

No, you absolutely don't need to be a professional speaker or actor to make functional, engaging, and dynamic presentations; but you will have to put in some serious work about how you conduct yourself and manage things if you expect to be taken seriously and be successful.

I wish I could remember who first taught me to treat a presentation or training session like a performance, because I owe that individual a heap of gratitude for doing so. The reason is simple. Once I understood that making presentations or conducting training sessions are in fact a form of "performance" on my part it didn't take a great leap of thought to understand that I had customers on the other end of the process. And when you have customers, you have a situation where you must focus on making them satisfied and want more. As an old sales geek myself, this line of thought came pretty darned easily.

So, if you take anything away from what I write in this Publication, please take the understanding that those you train are your customers, and as such they deserve the very best effort on your part each and every time when they visit you for the training you are offering them.

Now you might ask just what exactly do I mean when I call training or making a presentation a performance, because you really don't have any lines or actions to memorize for the script. Right? Wrong... because you do have lines to memorize and actions to consider if you expect to make your presentations lively, credible, and engaging. And, most of what we will discuss throughout the rest of this Publication is designed to help you understand that this is so, and to identify what you need to do to be successful in making it happen.

Yes making a training presentation is in fact a performance, because you do very definitely have a script to learn. We just call it the training content in our business. It's a performance because you have required actions to consider based on the nature of the presentation and room set-up you are working with. And, you have to manage yourself well in the process and be prepared to respond to the other actors and actresses in the room (your student participants) just like the performer does on stage when the camera is running. And then, just like the performer, you have to have a plan in mind for when things get a little squirrelly because they will at times.

So, at the end of the day the instructor /trainer is indeed a performer who must get prepared for the show by practicing his or her script, be ready to look "perfect" for the camera, know when and how to deliver his or her lines, and know what actions to take in order to be successful and ultimately make the participants want to come back for more.

There are a few simple skills that even the occasional presentation instructor can rely on to help make sure that the presentation material get's delivered in a manner that's effective and dynamic. I refer to these as engaging the audience...

YOU ENGAGE YOUR AUDIENCE WITH

Your Feet
Your Voice
Your Hands
Your Eyes
Your Ears
Your Body Language

Your Feet
Your feet can be a very useful tool so long as you use them with a purpose. They are especially useful when the room set up is such that you have participants all around you for example. It's important, however, that you move with a purpose to engage the group or specific individuals rather than random nervous skittering around. It is acceptable to stand in one place so long as you engage the group and use other methods to maintain a dynamic presence, such as your tone of voice or hand movement to make your points. The one thing you must avoid is moving in such a way that your back is turned to any part of the group for any length of time.

Your Voice
Your voice is the single most effective tool you have to manage the presentation and ensure that it remains dynamic and interesting. First of all, you must always be ready to speak loud enough for everybody to hear and clear enough so that all can understand what you say. If you need to use a microphone to enhance the volume of your voice, be prepared to do so. Do not! Let me repeat - do not allow your voice to fall into a monotone either by being too low and slow or too loud and rapid. You need to modulate your voice up and down, and change the pace of your speaking to keep the room engaged. This is important folks, and takes a little practice to perfect. The combination of moving around the room and changing the pace of the volume and speed of your speaking are very effective ways to keep the interest and attention up.

Your Hands

Be careful how you use your hands. We will talk about "nervous ticks" in a later chapter, but suffice it to say that your hands are the culprits for many of the mistakes made by presenters. I always recommend that you take everything out of your pockets so that you have nothing that your grubby fingers want to reach for and grab. There's nothing more distracting to a group than an instructor who's constantly putting his or her hands in the pockets or messing with the buttons on their shirt while speaking. Likewise you will want to avoid distractions like brushing at your hair or twirling your pen. You also want to avoid what can appear to be aggressive motions with your hands, unless pointing or waving serves a specific purpose in the presentation. It's far less threatening to an individual if you engage them with a friendly opened hand rather than a pointed finger. The open hand serves as an invitation while the pointed one appears to be a challenge. Hand motions as you speak can be very engaging if done in a careful, purposeful, and inviting manner.

Your Eyes

For the most part you will use your eyes to help you manage the room and pay attention to what's going on and how the group is responding to your presentation. Take advantage of doing so and be prepared to change things up when you see that things might be lagging or you're losing the attention of a few. Much like your hands and feet, you will also want to use your eyes to engage individuals through direct eye contact, especially once you determine who your friends are in the room. Be careful to share your eye contact with the entire group as you do.

Your Ears

Pay attention to what you hear, both from your own voice and the comments being made around the room. What you hear from participants will help you determine how your presentation is being received. And, just as important listening to what's going on will also allow you to stop side conversations from disrupting your presentation.

Your Body Language

Your body language is important and you must always make sure that it's presenting a positive message. Never allow your body language to show any form of frustration, disappointment, or anger when you present. In a "difficult room" you certainly don't want to become part of the problem.

So, as you can see you have a wide variety of tools available to you to use when conducting a training course or making a presentation. The essential point however, is that regardless which of your physical assets you use or how you use them, you must always do what's both comfortable for you and fits the style and nature of the presentation you are planning.

In the business world it's common that we not just invite employees to participate in the training and information gathering sessions we schedule, we typically require their attendance. This is an important point, because it's my firm opinion that especially when you require individuals to attend a "performance" **you owe it to them to do your very best to insure that it's worth their time.**

What do we mean by this do you ask? It's simple, because time is valuable in business and when it comes to your employees you are typically paying for it in any case. It's important that you be both efficient and dynamic with the time you ask employees to invest in the training presentations you invite them to. Personally, I feel that any session you ask employees to attend should pass what I call the "credibility test"

Presentation Credibility Test

Is it a required part of their job?
Is it relevant to what they do?
Does it include information they need to do their jobs?
Will the information be career enhancing?
Will the presentation be efficient and dynamic?

Is it required?
Some training presentations are simply required, either by government mandate or the policy and benefits offered requirements of the organization. When it comes to the EPA, OSHA, or essential Policies and Procedures the company owes it to it's employees to share the information, but also owes it to them to do so in a time efficient manner that doesn't waste time away from productive endeavors.

Is it relevant?
If it's not required by policy or law, the training you offer absolutely must be relevant to what the invitees do so you don't risk it being a complete waste of time. And to make a presentation relevant, regardless the subject content, it's essential that you, the instructor, attach what's being presented to the real world of the employees invited to the session.

Does it include information they need to do their jobs?
This is a continuation of our discussion about relevance. The key here is that the subject matter has information of value to the jobs being performed and is current in all of the processes and procedures included in the training presentation.

Will the information be career enhancing?
Any information that isn't directly relevant to current jobs or to specific policy requirements should be career enhancing not to risk becoming a waste of time.

Will the presentation be efficient and dynamic?
This is as important, if not more so, than all of the other credibility tests. Many times you, the instructor, don't have much control over what you're asked to train or present, but you do have control over how you do it and how long it takes.

I also have 4 rules that I go by for those preparing to make training presentations to employees, which are as follows:

(1) Carefully <u>review the information</u> to be shared to have it well in mind
(2) Become the <u>subject expert</u> for the training content if at all possible
(3) Review the presentation so you <u>know it completely</u>
(4) <u>Practice</u>, <u>practice</u>, and <u>practice</u> some more what you plan to say

As I say repeatedly, detailed preparation is the key to a great presentation, regardless the subject matter. I once had a training professional tell me that a presenter needs to practice no less than 6 hours for every hour of presentation he or she plans to do. While this level of preparation may not always be possible in our corporate environment where tight schedules are the rule, the 6 to 1 ratio does make an important point about what it takes to be well prepared. Remember: the more you prepare and practice, the better the presentation will be, and the greater will be the results. I guarantee it!

So, what exactly do we mean by being well prepared? Like our previous discussion about our training presentations being in fact a performance, we now want to focus on the 2 essential elements of any presentation. The first is the subject matter content itself, and the second is the presentation. These are the "what" and "how" of what you plan to present during the session, and it's important that you concentrate on both.

The content: This is the what you are going to present
Frankly, there's no substitute or shortcut when it comes to knowing the content of what you plan to present. **And, there's no worse "sin" that a presenter can commit than failing to become an expert on the content.** This may not require that you be a complete "subject expert" in every case, but it does require a firm knowledge of the information in general for what you plan to share with those you invite to train. Not only does this require practice on the part of the instructor, but it may also require some research with those who are the real subject experts.

The presentation: This is the how you will be presenting it
Once you have familiarized yourself with the content to your satisfaction, it's now time to get familiar with the presentation, whatever that may be. Typically, in today's world it's likely to be on a Microsoft Power Point template, which will require you to do 2 things; be completely familiar with how power point works so you can manage the presentation properly, and become familiar with how the subject matter is broken down in the presentation. **The second greatest "sin" of the presenter is to not be familiar enough with the presentation that you get off track and present the subject matter in the wrong sequence.** Doing so becomes confusing to the audience and you risk being redundant with information that's repeated unnecessarily.

After you've completed your due diligence so that you have the subject and presentation content well in mind, I'm a huge fan of the **"dress rehearsal"** where you either get a few associates into a room (preferred) or do the presentation from beginning to end into the mirror. There's no substitute for actually having to voice what you intend to say, and frankly it will also help you with some of the actions we've previously discussed that you will use. For additional information regarding this subject, refer to the chapter on Power Point.

How many times have you come into a training room at the scheduled time, only to see the instructor frantically trying to get his or her act together with the equipment, causing the session to start 15 minutes late or more. **THIS IS UNCALLED FOR AND COMPLETELY UNACCEPTABLE!**

I have one rule, and one only, that applies here; which is that you must know how to use the equipment that you plan to rely on for your training presentation and you need to arrive **no later than an hour before** the scheduled start of the meeting to make sure everything works right.

And what this means if you plan to give a power point based presentation, is that you will need to have the following:

A laptop computer with the presentation already loaded
And if not, a stick drive with the presentation
A projector that you know how to use
Power and extension cords for the laptop and projector
A presentation screen
Speakers if there is to be audio in the presentation
A remote clicker to manage the presentation (optional)

You need to arrive in the room in time to get everything hooked up and make sure that it all works correctly (ideally you will have already checked in advance to make sure you have everything you will need or maybe you are just lucky enough that you can rely on an IT department to assist you). When the meeting's supposed to start is not the time to discover that you don't know how to use the projector, the speakers will not interface correctly with your laptop, or discover that your extension cord is too short to reach the closest outlet.

And, before your invitees begin to arrive it's important that you do a final check to make sure the room set up is as it should be for how you plan to present the material to your audience and that you are ready with any support materials to be handed out.

We've talked previously about your image and the actions you plan to take during your presentation, so we won't take any more time with them at this point. What we will discuss is how you manage yourself during the presentation so that you make sure you stay on task and on time. This is often referred to as Emotional Intelligence.

Time is the enemy you must control
We've said it before and we'll say it again, that when you invite employees or require them to take time out of their schedule to spend time with you, you owe it to them to be efficient in how you use it. It's not only inefficient, but it's highly disrespectful to do otherwise, and at the end of the day it's in your hands to control the situation. And, there are 2 things you need to do:

1) Meetings must always start and end on time where possible, excepting those cases where things happen that are out of your control. We talked about showing up early so that you can be sure to start on time. It's just as important that you manage your presentation so that you end on time.

   And, how do you do this - with a presentation outline of course! Remember when we discussed doing a full practice presentation earlier? Well, this is the time to create a **"timed outline"** for the presentation so that you can keep yourself on task while presenting it. This is an important tool that lets you know where you stand throughout your performance. A favorite strategy that I use on occasion is to have a volunteer in the audience be in control of the time, and keep me posted how I'm doing.

2) And, this leads to my second point, which is that you need to stick to the script so that you don't go into irrelevant tangents that use up the time you have. I've actually seen presenters who don't discipline themselves well, and end up spending precious time talking about nonsensical side issues causing the meeting to run into overtime. Again, this is another reason why it's important that you practice your presentation and take notes about any added information you plan to insert into the discussion.

Why they call it emotional intelligence

Take note: No presentation ever goes exactly the way you plan. There will be issues that come up; either with the subject matter or the equipment that will force you to make adjustments. There will also be times when the group takes the discussion in an unexpected direction. You want to be prepared for this eventuality. But, what you really need to be prepared for is when the group reacts negatively to the presentation.

Maybe it's a tough crowd, or maybe there are a few bad actors. Maybe the group is just having a tough day, or quite possibly the information you are sharing is difficult and hard to accept - harassment training for example. This is where it becomes critical that you stay in control of your own emotions so that you can both control the room and move the discussion in a positive direction. Here are some pointers:

- Never get combative or defensive about a negative reaction
- Don't stifle discussion unless absolutely necessary - direct it instead
- Have the answers prepared for the likely hard questions or concerns you can expect to receive
- Seek your "friends" and isolate your "enemies" to help manage the conversation

Remember: It's your show and your responsibility to control the room, so don't let somebody else take it over.

Handling "Nervous Ticks"

Nervous Ticks are the unconscious actions we all take when we get nervous or uncomfortable, and we all have them regardless of our skill or level of experience. My nervous tick is that I tend to rock on my feet or direct my attention to the left side of the room and unfairly ignore the right. Common ones are "and ummm" or finishing sentences with "okay" as well as some of the things we mentioned earlier in our discussion such as fiddling with pens, putting hands in pockets, etc. It's important that you identify your nervous ticks and work to limit them as much as you can during a presentation. This takes both awareness and practice.

It's all in your hands

Nobody but you is in charge and it's entirely in your hands to make the session a positive or negative one for the participants, and staying in control of yourself and all of the actions you take is the first and most important step in doing so. This takes practice, experience, and confidence to achieve. But, over time with work and effort I promise that you will be able to manage even the most difficult situations.

Managing the Room

What do we mean by "managing the room?" What we mean is that there are a number of aspects involving the room itself that any instructor / trainer must consider and manage if he or she is to have a smooth and efficient presentation. For our discussion about the room we will assume that you have the equipment you need (computers, projectors, screens, etc.) on hand based on our discussions in a previous chapter. At the risk of being overly redundant, however, let me just say that you need to make absolutely sure that you have all that you need to complete your presentation before you begin your preparations, and making sure you have all you need **means arriving early enough to really make sure and be fully prepared**. The following are what you need to consider in terms of room management:

- How the room is set-up is a key consideration for room management and something that needs to be given much thought before the presentation. There may be times where you have no ability to determine the set-up, and when that's the case you have to plan accordingly. But, where you do have the ability to determine the set-up (a classic instructional classroom, group tables, "U" shape, etc.) it's something you must think about.

  Room set-up preferences are determined by the nature of the presentation and your presentation style. If it's an instructional presentation and you are more comfortable in one spot at a podium or such, then the classic classroom may be the obvious choice. The presentation content might be one that includes a lot of group activities, and when this is the case a set-up of group tables might be more suitable for your purposes. Personally, I like to be able to move around and engage the group as I present, so where the room allows I prefer a "U" shape set-up where I can roam around and speak directly to individuals. Whatever your preference or requirements, the room set-up should be given serious consideration before you start.

- Privacy is sometimes an issue where the room is either part of a corporate office or a meeting room in a hotel or conference center. Don't forget to close doors so that there are no unnecessary distractions from outside the room during your presentation. You might even put a sign on the door.

- Be sure you know the exit doors and rest room locations so that you can share them with the participants before you start your meeting session.

- In today's world where smoking isn't allowed in most buildings, you will want to share the outside locations for doing so with those who will want or need to smoke during breaks.

- At those times when your sessions are scheduled to last more than an hour, I strongly suggest that you include breaks in your plan outline so that your participants can get out of their seats, stretch their legs, and take a break if needed. Doing so will help keep their attention.

- Lunches are required for meetings that last over 4 hours by mandate of the Department of Labor and must be planned for accordingly. So, you need to have a plan for lunch that includes the number of participants you expect and how you plan to have it delivered when this is the case.

- A clock located someplace where you can see it will help you stay on track with your presentation. You're right I'm anal, but I can tell you from my own experience that employees truly appreciate it when you value their time and keep things on track.

- Engaging individual participants during your presentation is one of the most effective ways to manage the room. Doing so can actually give those attending a form of personal ownership in the proceedings, which in itself can prevent the potential issues or mischief that can sometimes take place.

- Change up activities are a great way to hold attention, especially when the session is going to be along one. These can range from ice breakers, relevant video presentations, to exercises that drive the subject matter home. A simple rule: Don't allow them to be too cutsie or time consuming. Change up activities can be a dangerous and unnecessary opportunity for wasted time if not managed well.

- Ice breakers in particular can be a wonderful tool to engage a group and change up the presentation. They should be quick, fun, but not overly cutsie in a way that provides a positive influence on the proceedings.

- Remember, you are in charge and it's your responsibility to manage the room in a way that insures a positive experience for all who attend the session.

- Lastly, don't be afraid to have fun. Fun is a valuable tool when used properly to engage the room and keep everybody interested in the subject matter of the day. Keep it lively but appropriate.

Much of this discussion involves the use of Power Point to deliver your presentation material, and we plan to discuss Microsoft Power Point in a later chapter, so we won't go into any great detail here about it. What we will discuss are some of the other technological issues you need to be aware and in control of to ensure a functional and effective training session.

- Let us repeat yet again that you must make sure that you have all of the equipment you need and know how to use it properly.
- If you are using a portable projector for your presentation, you need to make sure of four things. (1) That you have a surface (table) to put it on. (2) Your table has room enough for your laptop computer with your program. (3) You have a long enough extension cord to reach your power source. And (4) You know how to run the projector.
- Always use a presentation screen. I've seen presentations done on a wall, and they are cheesy and sometimes ridiculously unreadable.
- A remote clicker is an effective tool to use to manage your slides (they only cost $30). But, here again, you need to practice to make sure you know how to use the clicker correctly so that you can advance, go back, or even point to a detail on the screen without problems.
- If you are using animations in your presentation, you will want to be absolutely familiar with where they are and what they include. If you don't, you risk getting out of sequence with your presentation.
- Remember the old saying: Lights, camera, action! It applies here when you plan to include video clips or movie presentations in your training. Remember when you plan to do so you will need to turn up and down the lights in the room. I recommend that you assign the task by getting a volunteer in the room to do it for you.
- One last note. Never allow a set-up to include extension cords running across the floor where you plan to stand and move during the presentation. Believe me when I say that tripping over a wire or pulling the laptop and projector off the table can be a distraction you don't need.
- Another recommendation I have is that, unless you are an expert or comfortable with all of the computer based systems you plan to use, try to have a back-up plan that includes a systems expert in case something does go completely wrong.

Remember Murphy's Law that says if it can go wrong, it will? Well guess what, no matter how hard you try to avoid them things do in fact go wrong and you need to be prepared with a plan for how you will respond if and when they do.

- Equipment breaks, so you need to consider what you might do if a stick drive with your presentation won't work anymore. The obvious choice here is to have a back up stick loaded with the presentation just in case.

- What do you do if the projector bulb all of a sudden flashes dark and won't work anymore? Projectors are expensive and you probably won't have a backup to rely upon, so what do you do now? This happened to me once and I was only able to do the presentation because I had hard printed copies of the power point and knew the material well so I could still present it.

- What if you do have a "bad actor" participant who no matter what you do won't cooperate? Remember, this is your meeting and you owe it to the rest of the group to handle the situation carefully. More important, you have to isolate a "bad actor" so he or she isn't allowed to take over control of your meeting. Don't get mad, just be politely insistent; but if it turns out you can't get the cooperation you need, you might need to ask the employee to leave the room. Be prepared to do so if need be.

- What if there are questions or concerns that you either just can't answer or don't have the time to address fully? First of all, there will be questions that you simply can't answer on the spot regardless how familiar you are with the subject matter, so you need to have an appropriate response in mind to address them when they come about. The best suggestion is to write the question down along with who asked it so that you can research the proper answer to be shared at a later date with both the individual who asked the question and the group as a whole.

Let me warn you that to promise to do so and not deliver is one of the cardinal sins of any training instructor.

And, there's a very effective strategy that I've learned called "The Parking Lot" for managing the questions and concerns that do come up...

Knowing that there will be unexpected questions that get asked or concerns about the subject matter is important. But, just as important is your strategy for how you will address them when they come about so that you don't side track or bog down your presentation. A practical and effective way to do so is what is often called the Parking Lot.

So, what is the Parking Lot...?

The Parking Lot is a place (typically a flip chart or white board) where you go by agreement of the entire group to list any questions or relevant concerns about the subject matter being presented that falls outside the parameters of the session itself. It may be a question that falls outside the specifics of the training, or one that requires more discussion than time allows. Or, it may be a concern brought up that risks a damaging (negative) discussion that needs to be set aside so that the session doesn't lose it's positive momentum. The solution is to write it down so that the instructor / presenter can either answer the question or concern in more detail after the session, or do the necessary research to find an answer.

Here's how it works...

- The group agrees at the suggestion of the instructor that the question or concern is a candidate for the "Parking Lot"

- The instructor writes the question or concern down along with the name of who brought it to the groups attention.

The non-negotiable rules of the Parking Lot...

- The instructor must determine what is required as a suitable response to the questions or concerns raised.

- The instructor must share a reasonable timeline for the expected response with the group.

- The instructor must honor his or her commitment to find the expected answer in the agreed upon timeframe and share it both with the individual and the group as a whole.

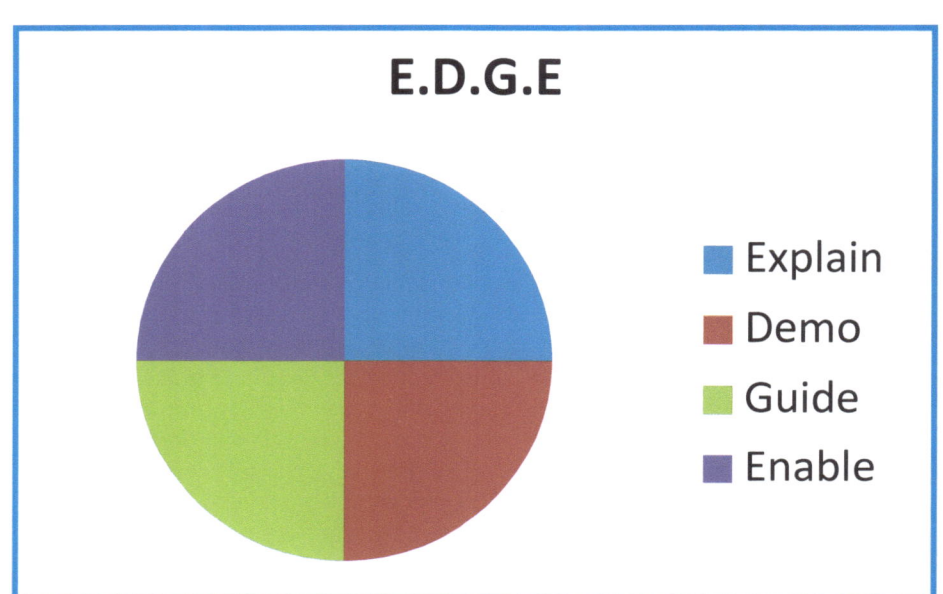

The E.D.G.E. acronym provides us the perfect visual picture for how individuals process information and learn. The process is simple: We first explain things, we then demonstrate what we mean, which is followed by some additional guidance to clear up any misunderstandings, and then we end up with demonstrative proof by the participant that he or she has received the information.

The E.D.G.E. acronym is certainly relevant and important to those who are designing and developing training materials, but it can be just as relevant to those tasked with presenting the material to others. This is especially true when working with tools such as power point or running a workshop type presentation session. And, it's certainly true when training new methods and procedures to employees.

Best of all, if you focus on the E.D.G.E. you will touch all three ways that individuals process information: Audio, Visual, and Physical. This is important because studies have shown that not all people learn and process information the same.

Some individuals either prefer or may even require that they receive information or new material in what we call an **"Audio"** fashion - by reading the information directly or being instructed by a classroom style teacher or instructor. Many times it will include a combination of reading and instructing. And, in some cases, this is all that's needed to get the message across.

Other individuals may both prefer or require that the information they need to learn and process be delivered and received **"Visually."** Visual methods can include anything from a bullet pointed power point presentation that highlights the key elements that must be understood and learned, all the way to video presentations that fully describe the subject matter. These may include:

- Pictures that show examples of the subject
- Graphics that give details about what the subject content is about

And then, there are those individuals who can't seem to process information well unless they actually get to touch and feel it. We often refer to these people as **"Hands-on"** physical learners. Hands-on learners do best when they get a chance to really touch things and get a feel for how they work. For these reasons, methods such as workshops work well, especially when the training involves such subjects as new products, processes, or new equipment.

The best instructional training will include a combination of **Audio, Visual, and Physical** techniques that not only address the varied way individuals process and learn information, but when you use all three methods you will most surely be following the E.D.G.E. explain, demonstrate, guide, and enable learning process.

A good example for how the E.D.G.E. philosophy is used during a presentation is a session that relies on power point as the visual framework for the instructional training. Here's how it can work...

- The power point slides provide a visual picture of the subject with both graphics and bullet pointed comments

- At the same time the instructor / presenter is providing the audio to the group by adding relevant details and explanations to what's being shown on the power point slides (this is why it's essential that the instructor does more than simply read the slides).

- Handouts, show and tell examples, and simple projects are excellent ways to provide the physical hands-on opportunities to drive the message home to the group.

It goes without saying that the Microsoft Power Point program is a powerful tool to use in developing and managing training programs. And, let me say from the beginning, that if you or your organization can afford to attend a professional instructional presentation on it's use, I would highly recommend that you do so.

Power Point is a developmental program template that allows you to create a presentation that's highly dynamic and very functional to use with groups to share information. Power Point lets you...

- Design or select a dynamic template to create your presentation material
- Be consistent in the size and shape (we call these fonts) of the language you plan to use
- Use pictures and graphics to further explain your subject content
- Use animations to control the presentation and make it interesting
- Use sound and video clips to make points and create additional interest

You may or may not be involved in the development of Power Point presentations, but if you are there are some "Do's" and "Don'ts" that you need to consider.

What to do when designing a Power Point presentation

It's important to remember what Power Point is designed to support and make more dynamic the material content you are presenting. Nothing more than that. A well designed power point presentation simply supports what you plan to say in a visual fashion. To do so there are some rules you should follow...

- **Be consistent in the Power Point slides that you use.** They should all have the same look and feel.
- **Be consistent in the fonts you use** for specific purposes, such as titles, bullet points, and detailed information.
- **Be consistent with the layout,** meaning where the wording is as compared to where you introduce pictures or graphics
- **Don't overdo the animations.** Animations are a great tool to use to control the presentation by not allowing the crowd to read ahead so that they have to pay attention to what you say.

If you concentrate on these simple rules when creating power point presentations they will be more professional in appearance and be easier for your participants to follow along in your presentation.

What not to do when designing a Power Point presentation
Conversely, many Power Point developers have a tendency to overuse the program and load it with too much information or have too many goofy cool things that only make it harder for the participants to follow along. Here are some things you should try to avoid...

- **Don't get too wordy.** Let me repeat this, power point is designed only to support what you say, not be the text of what you say. If you get too wordy, the students are struggling to read the slides instead of listening to what you say. "Think bullet points"
- **Don't jump around with the template.** Be consistent in what you do. If you have word content on one side of the screen and pictures on the other, stick with that on every slide. This makes it easier for your participants.
- **Don't overdo the animations**. Animations should only be used to control the presentation, and overusing them to be cool only makes it more difficult for the participants. If you use "fly-ins" or "slide-ins" or "simple appearance" animation tools, use what you choose for every slide unless you have a specific reason to change.

Some useful hints when using a Power Point presentation

- **Get familiar with the material on the slides!** The worst thing you can do is stand before a crowd of fellow employees with your back turned reading from the screen because you don't know what's coming.
- **Get a remote clicker to go from screen to screen.** Believe me, it's much easier and much more professional to have one than to have to run to a laptop every time you need to advance to the next slide (unless of course you have a person to serve as your engineer to manage the show).
- **Be careful about having participants read the slides.** While some instructors are big fans of this approach, I'm not. To me it's a much less efficient approach that puts undue stress on members of the group. There are other much more effective ways to engage the participants in what you are doing. Some of these we discussed earlier in our "managing the room" conversation.

When designing and using Power Point I tend to use the old KISS principle (keep it simple stupid). If you do, then your presentations will be more efficient, effective, and dynamic. Remember: You are the show, not the power point presentation.

Other useful Power Point capabilities

Power Point offers tools to the presenter / instructor in addition to the presentation slides created to manage a training session. These include:

- **Outline format:** The outline format takes your presentation and organizes it in an outline that provides the perfect template to use to create the timed outline we discussed in an earlier chapter. By clicking on the "View" tab at the top of your Power Point menu, then clicking on "Outline format" it will pull up the screen that you can then print.

- **Notes page:** This is a great format that the presenter instructor can use either to help with his or her own presentation, or as an additional tool to the participants to share additional information. The notes page is at the bottom of each presentation screen where you can enter additional information or notes about what you intend to say or emphasize. To access the note page format you click on the "View" tab, go to "Notes page" where you see that your power point slide shows above your notes in a nifty easy to use form for you and your students. If used to its full extent, Notes Page can actually help you create a guidebook or instructional manual that aligns and follows your presentation exactly.

- **Handout master:** Need a workbook for your presentation? Handout master allows you to take the slides and organize them in a handout (slides only) or workbook (slides with spaces for notes) fashion so you can provide them to the participants if needed or desired. It's accessed by going to the "View" tab, click on "Handout master" and make your selections for the format you want.

Once again, I can't emphasize enough what a powerful and useful tool Microsoft Power Point is, and if used properly and efficiently will serve your needs greatly. And, I do recommend that it's money well spent to take a course or get some expert instruction in its use and capabilities.

Whether they be Citrix based GoToMeeting / GoToWebinar, Google Hang-out, or some other internet based group meeting program there are some specific things you must know to prepare for, conduct, and manage the training sessions you plan.

- First of all you will need to set up an account with the proper access as an instructor with the vendor (Citrix, Google, etc.) that you select for the platform you plan to use.

- You will then need to familiarize yourself with the processes used to set up meetings, invite participants, then manage the sessions themselves.

And, just like you must in any training presentation you do, you have to become completely familiar with the material that you plan to present.

Even more so than when you do a classic power point based presentation face to face with a group of participants, conducting an internet based off site meeting with participants is very much like a performance, and you must conduct yourself as a performer sitting in a studio while doing so.

The various platforms offered by Citrix, Google, and others all allow you to monitor who is present in the meeting, but most don't allow much direct interaction between you and the participants (Google Hang-out is the exception). Some, such as GoToMeeting, do provide the ability to interact by way of survey questions and back channel messaging. Some also allow for post session testing or surveying.

What every platform does do is allow you to share a power point presentation as well as related files and information by way of your computer screen. Your participants can log into the session on an internet connected computer and see and hear what you are presenting.

For more information and details regarding how to properly conduct an internet based remote training session with participants in various off site locations you should refer to the *TRAIN2WIN* **How To Conduct An Effective Webinar** publication which is also available for purchase on Amazon.com.

Helpful hints for setting up and conducting Webinar training presentations...

- Select the vendor with a platform that best offers what you need for your presentations. This may be based on what's available to you through your company or organization.

- Make yourself entirely familiar with all of the processes for scheduling a session, inviting participants, and managing all of the processes necessary to conduct a webinar based session.

- Most vendors offer the ability to conduct practice sessions to better familiarize yourself and resolve issues before doing the official session with invited participants. Take advantage of this.

- **REMEMBER...** conducting a webinar training session is much like doing a performance without an audience present, so it's absolutely essential that you become intimately familiar with the content you plan to present and how you plan to do so.

- As the presenter / instructor it will be your responsibility to not only do the presentation itself, but you will also have to manage the various required processes during the session. To make it easier to do so, I strongly recommend that you use a **Headset and microphone** set instead of the telephone based connection for your voice and sound. Doing so frees up your hands to manage what you need to do both on screen and with any related paperwork or notes that you may have to help conduct the session.

- **PREPARATION...** preparation is key if you want your session to be problem free and as efficient as possible for your participants. You will want to log on no later than 15 minutes (I do 30) before the scheduled start of the session to ensure at you have everything ready to go when they start logging on.

- You should have all of the presentation materials (power point in many cases), related files opened and minimized at the bottom of your computer screen ready for use during the presentation, and be sure to practice how you plan to bring them up onto the screen and use.

- Plan to conduct your session in a location where you will have the fewest distractions possible. You don't want the phone ringing in the background or people trying to get your attention while you are conducting a session.

Not any one of us can expect to be a seasoned presenter / instructor our first time out, but if we rely on effective feedback to identify our potential areas of improvement we can expect to enhance our skills much quicker.

And, here's how you do so...

- Every presentation you make should include a survey at the end that asks relevant questions about the quality of your performance which should include the following. And you should ask for specific performance standards such as "Poor" for less than average or good, "Average" for an okay performance, and "Above Average" for better than expected. I prefer written surveys that require comments rather than the check the box type.

- Over-all impressions of the presentation

- Was the instructor / presenter on time and ready to go at the scheduled time?

- Did the session offer new ideas, knowledge, or skills that will help you with your job performance?

- How would you rate the instructor / presenter?

- What areas did the instructor / presenter exceed your expectations (be specific)?

- What areas did the instructor / presenter not meet your expectations (be specific)?

- Can you name some specific ways the instructor / presenter can improve in the future?

Remember though, surveys are a useless waste of time if you don't plan to review them and take to heart the things written, especially areas of potential improvement. I like to ask that participants sign their surveys for the simple reason that I might choose to contact them for further discussion where applicable and desired.

TRAIN2WIN Presentations Self Check

	YES	NO
(1) I know the material well that I plan to present & train	☐	☐
(2) I'm fully familiar with the method of presentation	☐	☐
(3) I've thoroughly practiced what and how I plan to present	☐	☐
(4) I have all of the needed equipment ready for use	☐	☐
(5) I've done a final check to insure everything works as it should for the presentation	☐	☐
(6) I have all of the related materials that I will need	☐	☐
(7) The room is set up and ready for participants to arrive	☐	☐
(8) I know bathroom and exit locations ready to share	☐	☐
(9) I have lunch / breaks set up where applicable	☐	☐
(10)I'm ready with answers to predicable questions / issues	☐	☐
(11)I have a timed outline to keep me on task & on time	☐	☐
(12)I have a back-up plan ready in case everything falls apart	☐	☐

There are no right answers to this self check, but it will hopefully give you an opportunity to work on the important aspects of doing presentations in a winning way that both supports your objectives and provides the training experience your participants are looking for.

TRAIN**2**WIN Publications

***TRAIN2WIN* Publications** are authored by Thom Mindala, President and CEO, and longtime training professional in the Paint and Coatings Industry. With a broad experience in employee based training initiatives and programs Thom brings a perspective to the consulting business that's both unique and dynamic.

Thom has a dedicated passion for the training process, especially as it relates to the business and corporate worlds. He's convinced that the frustration that so many organizations experience when they undertake the training process with their members is not only solvable, but unnecessary.

If you have questions or comments about this or any other *TRAIN2WIN* Publication, you can direct them to Thom personally using one of the following methods:

Telephone: 303-947-8989

Email: TMindala@gmail.com

Website: Train2win.weebly.com

If you would like to know more about Thom's training philosophy or about *TRAIN2WIN*, you can purchase a copy of the *TRAIN2WIN* **Manifesto** or the *TRAIN2WIN* **Presentation Guide** on Amazon.com. The Manifesto spells out in detail Thom's entire philosophy about training, and how it should and can work. The Presentation Guide details much of his philosophy while explaining the wide range of training opportunities that *TRAIN2WIN* offers it's clients.

www.ingramcontent.com/pod-product-compliance
Lightning Source LLC
Chambersburg PA
CBHW050918290526
45792CB00002B/800